Table Of Contents

Jalapeño Meatballs with Potatoes 47

Beef Taquitos 49

Ground Beef Stir Fry 51

Beef Fajitas 53

Roast Beef 55

Beef Chili 57

Pepper Pork Chops 59

BBQ Pork Strips 62

Honey Mustard Pork Balls 64

Char Siu Pork 66

BBQ Pork Ribs 68

Seafood

Salmon Pasta with Rosemary Tomato Sauce 70

Shrimp Green Curry Noodles 73

Salmon with Potatoes, Fennel and Dill 76

Rosemary Garlic Prawns 79

Black Cod 81

Vegetarian

Cauliflower Burger 83

Vegetable Pasta Salad 86

Buffalo Cauliflower 88

Baked Sweet Potato 90

Pita Bread Pizza 92

Air Fryer Useful Tips

1. Start with carefully reading the instructions for your device

Every air fryer comes with a manual that you should carefully study, as it contains useful tips and all the needed information on how to use it safely.

2. Mix and shake well

If you want to cook with minimum oil you should remember that there will be no liquid that helps your food to mix properly. Thus, it is important to shake the fryer at least once during the cooking process. The best option is to shake your food at the midway point.

3. Use at least a small spoon of oil

Some air fryers do not need oil at all, but still it is recommended to use at least 1 teaspoon of oil for cooking. It will make your food even tastier but no less healthy.

4. Use cooking spray

If you do not want to use oil at all try cooking sprays. They are not very expensive and will definitely help you to get better cooking results as well as keep your air fryer in good condition.

5. Do not overcrowd your air fryer

If you overcrowd the air fryer it can lead to technical problems and damages. Besides, it will take more time to cook the food evenly. This recipe book gives you details on how to put the food into the air fryer so you do not have to worry about anything, just follow the steps.

6. Do not remove your food immediately

Let your food dry a bit in the air fryer before removing it. The air fryer processes differ from those of the oven or a microwave and that it why you should follow some specific rules to get the best result.

7. Bring products to room temperature

If you take the ingredients out of the fridge it would be better if you let them cool down to a room temperature. It will reduce the cooking time and make the food even crispier.

8. Not only frying

You can use your air fryer not only for frying; it has much more useful functions. You can cook lasagna, noodles, pizza and cakes in it. In this book you will find a great variety of healthy recipes for your everyday meal.

Chicken Kiev

Servings: 2
Cooking Time: 25 minutes
Calories: 479 kcal

Ingredients

 2 medium chicken breasts
 3.5 oz garlic and herb flavor cream cheese
 ¼ teaspoon garlic paste
 2 sprigs fresh parsley
 1 medium egg
 2.6 oz breadcrumbs (or make your own with
 two slices of bread)
 salt and pepper, to taste

Instructions

1. Preheat the air fryer to 350°F.
2. Remove parsley leaves from their stems.
   Discard the stems and roughly chop the leaves.
   If you don't have fresh parsley you can use 1 tsp
   of dried parsley instead.

3. Mix cream cheese with garlic paste and half of chopped parsley in a medium bowl.
4. Use a rolling pin and flatten chicken breasts a bit.
5. Using a sharp knife, make a small horizontal cut in every chicken breast; try not to cut all the way through.
6. Open one chicken breast and carefully pour half of the cheese mixture into it. Repeat for the second portion.
7. If you are making your own breadcrumbs, place two slices of bread into the blender and pulse until crumbs are formed.
8. Mix the breadcrumbs, remaining parsley, salt and pepper in a large bowl. In a separate bowl, beat an egg with a fork.
9. Dip chicken breast into the egg, making sure to coat it as much as possible. Then roll chicken in breadcrumbs until totally covered. Make sure you hold the chicken together so the cheese doesn't fall out. Repeat for the second portion.
10. Wrap chicken breasts in silver foil and put into the air fryer. Cook for 25 minutes.
11. Check if the chicken is cooked by making sure there is no pink meat.
12. Serve the chicken straight from the air fryer with baked chips and a salad.

Lemon Pepper Chicken

Servings: 2
Cooking Time: 16 minutes
Calories: 331 kcal

Ingredients

   2 medium chicken breasts
   4 unwaxed lemons
   2 tablespoons Chicken Seasoning (if you can't
   find Chicken Seasoning in your local store you
   can crumble 2 chicken stock cubes in a bowl
   and mix with 2 tsp dried parsley)
   2 teaspoons garlic paste
   salt and pepper, to taste
   1 spring fresh parsley, chopped (optional)

Instructions

1. Preheat the air fryer to 350°F.
2. Remove rind from lemons using the smallest grating surface of your grater and set it aside. Then juice lemons into a small bowl.
3. Mix lemon juice, lemon rind and garlic paste in a bowl.
4. Prepare two pieces of silver foil, one for each chicken breast. The foil should be big enough to wrap the meat.
5. Season both sides of the chicken breast with salt and pepper. Rub chicken breasts with Chicken Seasoning until it changes color slightly.
6. Place the chicken portions onto the foil.
7. Pour lemon mixture over chicken breasts.
8. Wrap the foil around chicken, making sure it's sealed up tightly. Use a rolling pin to flatten the portions slightly to get even more flavor.
9. Put chicken into the air fryer and cook for 16 minutes.
10. Check if the chicken is cooked by making sure there is no pink meat.
11. Sprinkle the chicken with chopped parsley.
12. Enjoy your chicken with vegetables or salad.

Chicken Fried Rice

Servings: 4
Cooking Time: 20 minutes
Calories: 787 kcal

Ingredients

8 oz white rice

8 oz frozen peas and carrots

8 oz chicken, boiled

1 small onion, diced

6 tablespoons soy sauce

1 tablespoons vegetable oil

Instructions

1. Cook rice according to the instructions on the packet, and allow to cool for 30 minutes.
2. Preheat the air fryer to 360°F.
3. Chop the cooked chicken into bite-sized pieces.

4. Mix cooked rice, vegetable oil and soy sauce in a big bowl. Combine well until rice absorbs liquid.
5. Add frozen vegetables, diced onion and cooked chicken to the bowl. Mix thoroughly.
6. Transfer rice mixture to the air fryer non-stick pan and cook for 20 minutes.

Chicken Kabobs

Servings: 2
Cooking Time: 15 minutes
Calories: 426 kcal

Ingredients

2 medium chicken breasts
3 bell peppers of different color, stem and seeds removed
6 mushrooms
5 tablespoons runny honey
5 tablespoons soy sauce
2 teaspoons oil
1 teaspoon sesame seeds
salt and pepper, to taste

Instructions

1. Preheat the air fryer to 338°F.
2. Cut chicken breasts into bite-sized squares. Put it into a medium bowl.
3. Season chicken with salt and pepper, add some oil.
4. Add honey and soy sauce to chicken. Mix well to make sure meat is fully covered. Add sesame seeds into the bowl and stir again. Set aside while you prepare vegetables.
5. Cut peppers into pieces roughly the same size as the diced chicken. Do the same with mushrooms (if you buy standard sized mushrooms you will just need to chop them in half).
6. Thread chicken and vegetables onto the wooden skewers, try to alternate meat and vegetables.
7. Once you've made all the kabobs, pour honey-soy sauce over them.
8. Load all the kabobs into the air fryer basket. Cook for 15-20 minutes. Check the chicken pieces are cooked well before serving.
9. Serve the kabobs on their own or with rice and salad.

Chicken Pie

Servings: 1
Cooking Time: 6 minutes
Calories: 751 kcal

Ingredients

    2 boneless chicken thighs
    5 mushrooms, sliced
    2 small potatoes, peeled and chopped
    1 onion, peeled and chopped
    1 carrot, peeled and chopped
    1 tablespoon oil
    1 tablespoon water
    2 sheets ready rolled puff pastry
    3 tablespoons milk
    2 teaspoons Worcestershire sauce
    1 teaspoon Italian mixed dried herbs
    1 teaspoon garlic powder
    1 teaspoon plain flour
    butter to glaze (optional)

salt and pepper, to taste

Instructions
1. Cut chicken into bite-sized pieces, season with salt and pepper.
2. Heat oil in a frying pan or wok. Add onion, carrot and potatoes. Cook on medium heat until vegetables soften and onion begins to turn translucent.
3. Add water to the pan. Add chicken cubes and mushrooms along with the dried herbs, garlic powder and Worcestershire sauce. Season well with salt and pepper.
4. Cook on medium heat until the chicken cubes are cooked through and there is no pink meat. Add plain flour into the pan and stir well.
5. Add milk and turn the heat up for the mixture to boil. Once boiled, reduce the heat and simmer until vegetables are soft.
6. Preheat the air fryer to 350°F.
7. Lay one sheet of pre-rolled puff pastry onto the air fryer nonstick baking tray. This will be the base of your pie. Use a fork to gently poke a few holes in the pastry.
8. Pour in the chicken mixture. Put second sheet of pastry on the top of a pie. Cut away the excess pastry, use a fork to press the edges and poke a few holes in the top.

9. Melt some butter and brush pastry with it (optional). This will make your pastry crispier and golden once cooked.
10. Put the pie in the air fryer and cook for 6 minutes until the pastry is golden brown.

Buttermilk Chicken

Servings: 4
Cooking Time: 20 minutes
Calories: 524 kcal

Ingredients

> 1.8 lb chicken thighs
>
> 16 oz buttermilk
>
> 3 teaspoons salt
>
> 2 teaspoons black pepper
>
> 1 teaspoon cayenne pepper
>
> 9 oz all purpose flour
>
> 1 tablespoon baking powder
>
> 1 tablespoon garlic powder
>
> 1 tablespoon paprika

Instructions

1. Rinse chicken thighs and pat dry with a paper towel. Place in a large bowl.

2. Season chicken with black pepper, cayenne pepper and salt.
3. Pour over the buttermilk. Make sure all chicken pieces are coated. Cover the bowl and refrigerate for at least 6 hours (or overnight).
4. Preheat the air fryer to 350°F.
5. Mix flour, baking powder, garlic powder, paprika and salt in a big bowl.
6. Take chicken out of the buttermilk mixture and dip each thigh in the flour. Make sure each piece is well coated. Shake off excess flour and put the chicken on a plate.
7. Put chicken into the air fryer basket skin side up. DO NOT STACK. Put the basket into the air fryer and cook for 8 minutes.
8. Remove chicken change sides. Put back into the air fryer and cook for another 10 minutes.
9. Place the chicken on paper towels to drain.

Smoked Paprika Chicken

Servings: 2
Cooking Time: 20 minutes
Calories: 344 kcal

Ingredients
    4 skin on chicken thighs
    3 teaspoons salt
    3 teaspoons garlic powder
    3 teaspoons dried parsley
    3 teaspoons smoked paprika

Instructions
  1. Preheat the air fryer to 350°F.
  2. Rinse chicken thighs and pat dry with a paper towel.

3. Mix salt, garlic powder, parsley and paprika in a bowl.
4. Rub chicken with the salt mixture.
5. Place chicken onto the fryer basket skin side is up. DO NOT STACK. Put the basket into the air fryer and cook for 8 minutes.
6. Remove the chicken and change the sides. Put back into the air fryer and cook for another 10-12 minutes until the chicken is cooked well and crust is formed.
7. Take the chicken out and place on paper towels to drain.

Orange Chicken Wings

Servings: 2
Cooking Time: 20 minutes
Calories: 414 kcal

Ingredients

6 chicken wings
1 orange
1 tablespoon sugar
1.5 tablespoon Worcestershire sauce
2   teaspoons dried country herb mix
salt and pepper, to taste

Instructions

1. Remove zest from the orange using the smallest grating surface of your grater and set it aside. Then juice the orange into a small bowl.
2. Rinse the chicken wings and pat dry with a paper towel. Place them into a big bowl.
3. Pour orange juice onto the wings. Add orange zest, sugar, Worcestershire sauce and herbs and rub the seasoning into the meat.
4. Cover and refrigerate for at least 30 minutes.
5. Preheat the air fryer to 350°F.
6. Place the foil into the frying basket, put the wings on it. Brush with half of the marinade and cook for 10 minutes.
7. Change the sides and brush with the rest of the marinade. Cook again for 10 minutes.
8. Serve with salad or vegetables.

Thai Chicken Curry

Servings: 4
Cooking Time: 20 minutes
Calories: 350 kcal

Ingredients

    1 lb chicken breast
    thumb sized ginger, peeled and minced
    1 garlic clove, minced
    1 jalapeño pepper, seeds removed, chopped
    1 medium red sweet pepper, stems and seeds removed, sliced
    1 medium green sweet pepper, stems and seeds removed, sliced
    1 medium zucchini, ends removed, sliced

8 oz light coconut milk
1 bunch fresh cilantro
2 teaspoons cornstarch
3 teaspoons mild Thai red curry sauce
salt and pepper, to taste
1 tablespoon canola oil
4 lime wedges (optional)

Instructions

1. Preheat the air fryer to 350°F.
2. Cut the chicken breast into thin strips. Put strips to the air fryer, add ginger, garlic and jalapeño. Season with salt and pepper and drizzle with ½ tablespoon canola oil. Cook for 8 minutes.
3. Remove chicken from the air fryer. Put sweet peppers, zucchini and another ½ tablespoon oil to the air fryer. Cook for 5 minutes.
4. Meantime mix coconut milk with the Thai sauce and cornstarch in a medium bowl.
5. Add the sauce mixture and chicken to the air fryer. Cook for 5-7 minutes, until the sauce thickens.
6. Roughly chop the cilantro and stir it into the cooked curry. Serve with rice and lime wedges.

Chicken Carrot

Servings: 2
Cooking Time: 25 minutes
Calories: 542 kcal

Ingredients
>2 medium chicken breasts
>1 carrot, peeled and thin-sliced
>1 lemon
>1 bunch of sage
>10 teaspoons butter
>salt and pepper, to taste

Instructions
1. Preheat the air fryer to 375°F.
2. Cut lemon in half. Cut the chicken breasts in half lengthways.

3. Cut 4 squares of parchment paper, big enough to wrap the chicken breasts. Make 2 two layered squares.
4. Place half of the sliced carrot on one parchment square and half on the other. Add 4 teaspoons butter to each square and season well with salt and pepper.
5. Lay two halves of chicken onto each pile of carrots. Place 2 sage leaves on top.
6. Squeeze half a lemon over each portion and add 2 more teaspoons butter to each portion, on top of the sage leaves.
7. Wrap the chicken and seal by folding the edges together. Repeat for the second square.
8. Put one parchment bag onto the baking tray in the air fryer and cook for 20-25 minutes, until the carrots are soft and the chicken is cooked well. Repeat for the second bag.
9. Serve the chicken on its own or with potatoes.

Teriyaki Chicken

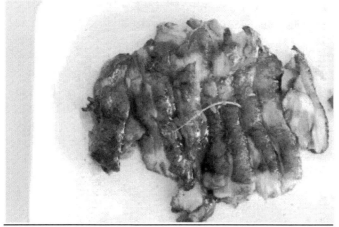

Servings: 4
Cooking Time: 20 minutes
Calories: 519 kcal

Ingredients

>   2 lb boneless, skinless chicken thighs
>   3 garlic cloves, peeled and crushed
>   5.3 oz low-sodium soy sauce
>   2 oz rice wine vinegar
>   3 tablespoons granulated sugar
>   1 tablespoons white wine
>   1 teaspoon sesame oil
>   ¼ teaspoon ground ginger
>   2 tablespoons cornstarch
>   2 tablespoons water

Instructions

1. Cut the chicken into 1 inch thick strips.
2. Mix garlic cloves, soy sauce, rice wine vinegar, sugar, white wine, sesame oil and ground ginger in a bowl.
3. Pour the sauce into a big freezer bag. Add the chicken pieces and mix to coat. Refrigerate for at least 4 hours to marinade.
4. Preheat the air fryer to 300°F.
5. Remove the chicken pieces from the bag, save the marinade for later. Put the chicken into the air fryer and cook for 15 minutes.
6. Mix cornstarch with water. Add the mixture to the marinade and stir to combine.
7. Pour the marinade-cornstarch mixture into the air fryer on top of the chicken and cook for another 3 minutes.

Panko Crumbed Chicken

Servings: 6
Cooking Time: 40 minutes
Calories: 407 kcal

Ingredients

6 chicken breasts

8 oz panko breadcrumbs

4.2 oz unsalted butter, melted

1 teaspoon salt

¾ teaspoon black pepper

½ teaspoon cayenne pepper

Instructions

1. Preheat the air fryer to 350°F.
2. Mix panko crumbs, cayenne pepper, ½ teaspoon salt and ½ teaspoon black pepper in a big, shallow dish or plate.

3. Mix melted butter, ½ teaspoon salt and ¼ teaspoon black pepper in a separate bowl.
4. Brush the butter mixture over the chicken breasts.
5. Dip two buttered chicken pieces into the panko mixture.
6. Put the chicken into the air fryer and cook for 15 minutes each side. For thinner chicken breasts you may only need 8 minutes per side.
7. Once cooked, let the chicken rest for 1-2 minutes before serving.

Chicken Satay

Servings: 2
Cooking Time: 15 minutes
Calories: 454 kcal

Ingredients

    1.1 lb chicken breast
    1 stalk lemongrass
    3 shallots, peeled
    3 garlic cloves, peeled
    3 teaspoons sugar
    1 teaspoon ground coriander
    1 teaspoon ground turmeric
    ½ teaspoon salt
    2 teaspoons olive oil
    1 tablespoon honey
    1 tablespoon vegetable oil

Instructions

1. Cut the chicken into long strips.
2. Remove and discard all but the white part of the lemongrass. Roughly chop the rest of it.
3. Using pestle and mortar pound the shallots, garlic and lemongrass into paste. Alternatively, you can use a blender.
4. Add salt, sugar, olive oil, coriander and turmeric to the paste. Mix to combine.
5. Put chicken pieces in a large bowl. Rub chicken with the paste. Cover the bowl and refrigerate for at least 4 hours or overnight to marinade.
6. Preheat the air fryer to 375°F.
7. Take the chicken pieces out of the bowl and thread the meat onto metal skewers.
8. Mix honey and vegetable oil in a small bowl. Brush the chicken skewers with honey mixture.
9. Place the skewers on the air fryer skewer rack and cook for 10-12 minutes until the meat is well cooked.

Turkey with Maple Mustard Glaze

Servings: 6
Cooking Time: 55 minutes
Calories: 436 kcal

Ingredients

    5 lb turkey breast
    1 teaspoon dried thyme
    1 teaspoon salt
    ½ teaspoon dried sage
    ½ teaspoon smoked paprika
    ½ black pepper
    2 oz maple syrup
    2 tablespoons mustard
    1 tablespoon butter

Instructions

1. Preheat the air fryer to 350°F.
2. Rub turkey breasts with olive oil.
3. Mix thyme, salt, sage, paprika and pepper in a small bowl.
4. Rub turkey with the spice mix.
5. Place turkey into the air fryer basket and cook for 25 minutes.
6. Change the side and cook for another 12 minutes. Flip it to the other side again and cook for another 12 minutes.
7. While the turkey is cooking, add maple syrup, mustard and butter to a small saucepan and cook over low heat until the butter is melted and the liquids are combined.
8. Once the turkey is cooked brush the maple syrup mixture all over it. Cook for a final 5 minutes until the skin is brown and crispy.
9. Remove the turkey from the air fryer and cover with foil; allow it to rest for 5 minutes. Slice and serve.

Turkey Calzone

Servings: 4
Cooking Time: 10 minutes
Calories: 1150 kcal

Ingredients

24 oz pre-made pizza dough
3 lb cooked turkey
4 tablespoons pizza or pasta tomato sauce
3.5 oz cheddar cheese, grated
1 oz mozzarella cheese, grated
1 oz back bacon, chopped
1 large egg
1 tablespoon tomato puree
1 teaspoon dried oregano
1   teaspoon dried basil
1 teaspoon dried thyme
salt and pepper, to taste

Instructions

1. Preheat the air fryer to 350°F.
2. Cut the dough into four 10 inch circles, to the size of small pizzas.
3. Mix and stir tomato sauce with oregano, basil and thyme in a small bowl.
4. Spread the tomato mixture onto each pizza base using a pastry brush leaving a 2.5 inch space at the edge of the dough.
5. Put turkey, bacon, cheddar and mozzarella onto one half of each base.
6. Beat the egg in a small bowl. Use some of the egg to brush the 2.5 inch gap you have left at the edge of each base.
7. Fold empty half of the dough over the filling so that the inside is completely covered. Press the edges together and then brush the remaining egg over the folded pizza.
8. Put calzones into the air fryer and cook for 10 minutes. You should be able to fit two calzones in the air fryer at once.

Beef Burgers

Servings: 4
Cooking Time: 10 minutes
Calories: 148 kcal per patty

Ingredients

    1 lb extra lean ground beef
    1 tablespoon Worcestershire sauce
    1 teaspoon Maggi seasoning sauce
    ½ teaspoon liquid smoke sauce
    1 teaspoon dried parsley
    ½ teaspoon dried oregano
    ½ teaspoon onion powder
    ½ teaspoon garlic powder

½ teaspoon salt
½ teaspoon black pepper
1 tablespoon oil

Instructions
1. Preheat the air fryer to 350°F. Spray/brush the air fryer tray with a little oil (if you're using the basket instead there's no need to use oil).
2. Mix Worcestershire sauce, seasoning sauce, liquid smoke, parsley, oregano, onion and garlic powders, salt and pepper in a small bowl.
3. Put ground beef into a large bowl and add the seasoning mixture. Mix well, but only until all the seasoning is well combined.
4. Split the beef into 4 pieces and shape each one into a burger patty. You should get a circle that's roughly 4 inches in diameter and about ¾ inch thick.
5. Place the patties into the tray and spray/brush with oil, cook for 10 minutes. If you prefer your burger well done, check after 10 minutes and cook for a little longer if needed.
6. Serve with buns and salad.

Beef Meatballs

Servings: 4
Cooking Time: 15 minutes
Calories: 468 kcal

Ingredients

    1 lb ground beef

    6 oz tomato ketchup

    3.75 oz brown sugar

    2 oz vinegar

    2 ½ tablespoons Worcestershire sauce

    1 tablespoon lemon juice

    1 tablespoon hot sauce (Tabasco)

    ½ teaspoon dried mustard

    3 ginger biscuits

Instructions

1. Preheat the air fryer to 375°F.
2. Crush the ginger biscuits by putting them in a small, sealable bag and applying pressure with a rolling pin.
3. Put the crushed biscuits into a big bowl. Add ketchup, brown sugar, vinegar, Worcestershire sauce, lemon juice, hot sauce and dried mustard and mix well.
4. Add the ground beef to the bowl and mix to ensure the meat is well coated.
5. Form medium sized beef meatballs; you should get 24 of them.
6. Place 12 meatballs at a time into the air fryer and cook for 15 minutes until the meatballs are cooked well and are crispy on the outside.
7. Serve with your favorite sauce or pasta.

Steak and Roast Potatoes

Servings: 2
Cooking Time: 30 minutes
Calories: 1029 kcal

Ingredients

2 striploin steaks
8 small potatoes
3 tablespoons olive oil
2 teaspoons cayenne pepper
2 teaspoons Italian dried herb mix
salt and pepper, to taste

Instructions

1. Preheat the air fryer to 350°F.

2. Wash potatoes and chop medium chunks (roughly in half). Put them in a medium bowl.
3. Add cayenne pepper, Italian herbs, salt, pepper and 2 tablespoons olive oil. Mix well.
4. Put potatoes into the air fryer basket and cook for 8 minutes. Toss the potatoes and then cook for another 8 minutes. Set aside once cooked and increase the air fryer's temperature to 390°F.
5. Rub the remaining oil, salt and pepper on both sides of the steaks.
6. Place the steak in the air fryer and cook for 7 to 13 minutes, depending on whether you prefer your meat rare or well done.
7. Serve with the roast potatoes.

Roasted Peppers stuffed with Beef

Servings: 2
Cooking Time: 20 minutes
Calories: 517 kcal

Ingredients

    8 oz lean ground beef
    2 medium green peppers, stems and seeds removed
    4 oz cheddar cheese, grated
    4 oz tomato Passata
    1 garlic clove, peeled and chopped

½ medium onion, peeled and chopped

1 teaspoon Worcestershire sauce

1 teaspoon olive oil

½ teaspoon salt

½ teaspoon black pepper

Instructions

1. Preheat the air fryer to 390°F.
2. Boil a small pan of salted water. Put peppers into the boiling water and cook for 3 minutes.
3. Heat oil in a small, nonstick pan. Add onion and garlic and cook on medium heat until they soften and brown. Remove from the heat and leave to cool for 5 minutes.
4. Mix the ground beef, cooked onion and garlic, Worcestershire sauce, 2 oz of tomato Passata, 2 oz of cheese, salt and pepper in a medium bowl.
5. Stuff the pepper hollows with beef mixture. Top each pepper with half of the remaining tomato sauce and cheese.
6. Put peppers into the air fryer basket and cook for 15-20 minutes until the meat is cooked and cheese is golden.

Jalapeño Meatballs with Potatoes

Servings: 4
Cooking Time: 35 minutes
Calories: 623 kcal

Ingredients

    16 beef meatballs (pre-made or cooked with our Beef Meatballs recipe)
    2 medium potatoes, cut them into bite size pieces
    1 large sweet onion, peeled and sliced
    1 jalapeño (or habanero) pepper, sliced
    1 sweet red pepper, stems and seeds removed, thin-sliced

1 sweet green pepper, stems and seeds
removed, thin-sliced
6 medium mushrooms, cut into quarters
5 tablespoons BBQ sauce
1 tablespoon olive oil
1 teaspoon garlic powder
salt and pepper, to taste

Instructions
1. Preheat the air fryer to 375°F.
2. Pour oil into the air fryer. Add potatoes and onions and cook for 15 minutes.
3. Add meat balls, jalapeño pepper, sweet red and green pepper, garlic powder, salt and pepper and cook for another 15 minutes.
4. Add BBQ sauce and cook for 5 minutes more.

Beef Taquitos

Servings: 6 people
Cooking Time: 6 minutes
Calories: 813 kcal

Ingredients

    1 lb lean ground beef
    1 lb cheddar cheese, grated
    18 extra thin corn tortillas
    1 small sweet onion, peeled and chopped
    ½ tablespoon garlic paste
    1 teaspoon cumin
    1 teaspoon ground coriander
    ½ teaspoon chili powder

salt and pepper, to taste

1   tablespoon oil

Instructions

1. Heat oil in a big frying pan. Add garlic and onions, cook until soften.
2. Add ground beef, cumin, coriander, chili powder, salt and pepper. Mix and cook until the meat is browned. Remove from the heat and set aside.
3. Preheat the air fryer to 370°F.
4. Warm the tortillas for 1 minute in the microwave.
5. Put some filling in the middle of each tortilla and top with a small handful of cheese. Make sure not to add too much filling.
6. Roll the tortillas into tubes. Use toothpicks to hold them together while they cook.
7. Put the rolled tortillas into the air fryer basket. DO NOT STACK. Spray/brush with a little oil.
8. Cook for 2 minutes before flipping the tortilla. Spray/brush the other side with a little more oil, then cook for another 4 minutes.
9. Remove the toothpicks and serve.

Ground Beef Stir Fry

Servings: 2
Cooking Time: 20 minutes
Calories: 702 kcal

Ingredients

    1.1 lb ground beef
    7 mushrooms, sliced
    2 garlic cloves, peeled and chopped
    1 onion, peeled and cut into wedges
    1 carrot, peeled and sliced
    1 white cabbage, shredded
    1 leek, sliced into rings
    1 apple, peeled and chopped
    2 tablespoons soy sauce
    1 ½ teaspoon salt
    1 teaspoon ground ginger

Instructions

1. Preheat the air fryer to 390°F.
2. Place the meet at the bottom of the air fryer pan. Put vegetables and an apple on top, and then add ground ginger and salt. Finally, pour the soy sauce on top.
3. Cook for 20 minutes until the meat is brown and cooked through.
4. Serve with rice.

Beef Fajitas

Servings: 2
Cooking Time: 10 minutes
Calories: 741 kcal

Ingredients

    1 lb beef steak, cut into strips
    1 green pepper, stems and seeds removed, sliced
    1 red pepper, stems and seeds removed, sliced
    1 white onion, peeled and sliced
    1 red onion, peeled and sliced
    1 serrano pepper, sliced
    2 tablespoons vegetable oil
    2 teaspoons salt
    1 teaspoon black pepper
    ½ teaspoon cumin
    1 teaspoon dried oregano
    1 teaspoon chili powder
    1 teaspoon garlic powder

6 corn or wheat tortillas
2 oz cotija cheese, shredded

Instructions

1. Preheat the air fryer to 390°F.
2. Mix salt, black pepper, cumin, oregano, chili powder and garlic in a medium bowl.
3. Pour vegetable oil in a separate bowl. Add dried spice mix and stir to combine.
4. Add the meat, all peppers and onions into oil and spice mixture. Mix well with your hands to coat.
5. Put a layer of foil on the air fryer basket. Put the spiced meat and vegetables on top. Cook for 5 minutes. Stir a bit and cook for another 4 minutes.
6. Remove the basket and prepare your tortillas. Put meat and vegetable mix in the middle of each tortilla and sprinkle with cheese.
7. Fold both sides of tortillas and secure with toothpicks if needed.

Roast Beef

Servings: 6
Cooking Time: 45 minutes
Calories: 362 kcal

Ingredients

    3 lb beef joint
    2 ½ tablespoons olive oil
    1 ¼ tablespoon paprika
    1 tablespoon salt (sea salt would work best)
    1 teaspoon garlic powder
    ½ teaspoon onion powder
    ½ teaspoon black pepper
    ½ teaspoon cayenne pepper

½ teaspoon dried oregano

½ teaspoon dried thyme

Instructions

1. Mix paprika, salt, garlic and onion powder, black and cayenne pepper, oregano and thyme in a small bowl. Add 2 tablespoons olive oil and stir well to combine.
2. Preheat the air fryer to 320°F.
3. Place the beef joint in a large bowl and add the remaining ½ tablespoon oil. Make sure all sides are covered.
4. Rub the beef with herbed oil mixture and spiced.
5. Wrap the joint in foil and put the meat into the air fryer. Cook for 30 minutes.
6. Change the side and cook for 15 minutes more.
7. If you prefer your meat well done cook for another 5 minutes.
8. Serve meat with steamed vegetables.

Beef Chili

Servings: 4
Cooking Time: 20 minutes
Calories: 364 kcal

Ingredients

    1.1 lb ground beef
    1 big onion, peeled and chopped
    1 garlic clove, peeled and chopped
    1 green pepper, stems and seeds removed, cut into chunks
    1 can chopped tomatoes
    1 can mixed beans in tomato sauce
    1 beef stock cube
    4 tablespoons concentrated tomato paste

½ tablespoon olive oil

2 teaspoons medium chili powder

1 teaspoon dried thyme

1 teaspoon dried oregano

1 teaspoon sugar

1 teaspoon salt

Instructions

1. Preheat the air fryer to 390°F.
2. Pour oil into the air fryer. Add onion, garlic, pepper and ground beef. Stir and cook for 5 minutes.
3. Add chopped tomatoes, beans, tomato paste, chili powder, thyme, oregano, sugar and salt. Add the beef stock cube, crumble and stir well. Cook 5 minutes.
4. Check if the beef is browned, add more salt if needed. Cook for another 3 minutes.
5. Serve with rice.

Pepper Pork Chops

Servings: 2
Cooking Time: 20 minutes
Calories: 577 kcal

Ingredients

    2 medium pork chops
    2 jalapeño peppers, stems removed, sliced
    2 spring onions, chopped
    1 egg white
    3.3 oz cornstarch
    2 tablespoons canola oil
    salt and pepper, to taste

Instructions

1. Slice the pork chops into large bites. You can either leave a bone or remove it. Pat dry the meat with paper towel.
2. Mix the egg white with ½ teaspoon salt and ¼ teaspoon black pepper. Beat until the mixture is foamy.
3. Put the pork in a big bowl and add the egg mixture. Cover the bowl and marinade in the refrigerator for at least 20 minutes.
4. Preheat the air fryer to 360°F.
5. Take the pork out of the refrigerator, add cornstarch and shake/stir until all the meat is thoroughly coated. Shake off any excess cornstarch.
6. Place the pork into the air fryer basket. Spray/brush with a little oil. Cook for 12 minutes making sure you shake the basket throughout.
7. Increase the air fryer temperature up to 400°F and cook for another 6 minutes until the pork is brown and crispy.
8. Meanwhile heat a frying pan and add a splash of oil into it. Add jalapeño peppers, spring onions, salt and pepper.
9. Cook on high heat stirring all the time to ensure it doesn't burn, for 1 minute.
10. Add the cooked pieces of pork to the pan and stir to coat them with the spring onions and

jalapeños. Stir for an additional minute to make sure the pork is covered with hot oil and vegetables.
11. Serve with rice.

BBQ Pork Strips

Servings: 6
Cooking Time: 20 minutes
Calories: 501 kcal

Ingredients

> 6 boneless pork loin chops
> 1 garlic clove, peeled and chopped
> 2 tablespoons soy sauce
> 2 tablespoons honey
> 1 teaspoon balsamic vinegar
> 1 inch piece fresh ginger (or ¼ teaspoon ground ginger)
> salt and pepper, to taste

Instructions

1. If you have fresh ginger, peel it and grate using the smallest grating surface.
2. Flatten the pork chops with a meat tenderizer. If you don't have a tenderizer you can cover the meat with a cling film and apply pressure using a rolling pin.
3. Season the flattened pork with salt and pepper.
4. Mix soy sauce, honey and balsamic vinegar in a small bowl.
5. Add garlic and ginger to the sauce mix. Stir well.
6. Place the pork chops into a large bowl and add the sauce, mix well. Cover and refrigerate for at least 2 hours.
7. Preheat the air fryer to 350°F.
8. Take the pork chops from the refrigerator and place into the air fryer baking tray, add some marinade juice. Cook for 5-8 minutes until one side is golden brown.
9. Flip the meat and cook for another 5-8 minutes until the whole chop is golden brown.
10. Remove the meat and cut into strips.

Honey Mustard Pork Balls

Servings: 4
Cooking Time: 15 minutes
Calories: 135 kcal

Ingredients

    10.6 oz ground pork
    half a small onion, peeled and chopped
    0.5 oz cheddar cheese, grated
    1 teaspoon garlic paste
    1 teaspoon runny honey
    1 teaspoon mustard
    1 basil bundle
    salt and pepper, to taste

Instructions

1. Preheat the air fryer to 395°F.
2. Remove and chop the basil leaves. Put the ground pork into a big bowl. Add onion, cheese, garlic paste, honey, mustard, basil, salt and pepper.
3. Form small sized meatballs. They should be a bit bigger than bite size.
4. Put the meatballs into the air fryer and cook for 14 minutes until the meatballs are lightly browned and well cooked in the middle.
5. Serve on their own or with mashed potato and vegetables.

Char Siu Pork

Servings: 4
Cooking Time: 50 minutes
Calories: 237 kcal

Ingredients

    4 boneless pork tenderloins

    5 oz dark muscovado sugar

    5 tablespoons soy sauce

    4 tablespoons hoisin sauce

    2 ½ tablespoons tomato ketchup

    2 ½ tablespoons sweet sherry

    2 ½ tablespoons runny honey

Instructions

1. Mix sugar, soy, hoisin, tomato ketchup, sherry and honey in a big bowl.

2. Cut the pork tenderloins in half and pat dry with a kitchen towel. Put the pork into a plastic freezer bag and seal it.
3. Carefully pour the marinade in the bag. Mix well to make sure the meat is coated. Refrigerate for at least 24 hours.
4. Preheat the air fryer to 420°F. Line the baking tray with tinfoil.
5. Put the pork onto the baking tray. Reserve the excess marinade and set aside.
6. Put the pork into the air fryer and cook for 15 minutes.
7. Reduce the air fryer temperature to 320°F and cook for another 25 minutes.
8. Increase the air fryer to 390°F and cook for a final 10 minutes, until the meat is dark on the outside and cooked in the middle.
9. Remove the pork and cut into thin strips.
10. Heat the reserved marinade in a pan on a low heat, or microwave it until thick and syrupy. Pour onto the meat or serve alongside.

BBQ Pork Ribs

Servings: 2
Cooking Time: 30 minutes
Calories: 791 kcal

Ingredients

    1.1 lb pork ribs
    3 garlic cloves, peeled and chopped
    4 tablespoons BBQ sauce
    1 tablespoons runny honey, and a little more for glaze
    1 teaspoon sesame oil
    1 teaspoon soy sauce
    ½ teaspoon five spice
    1 teaspoon salt
    1 teaspoon black pepper

Instructions

1. Wash the pork ribs. Cut the rack into small portions and place into a big bowl.
2. Mix garlic, BBQ sauce, honey, sesame oil, soy sauce, five spice, salt and pepper in a medium bowl.
3. Pour the sauce mix over the ribs and stir well to make sure they are fully covered.
4. Cover and refrigerate for at least 4 hours to marinade.
5. Preheat the air fryer to 350°F.
6. Put the ribs into the air fryer. Cook for 15 minutes.
7. Slightly coat the ribs with honey using a brush. Flip the meat and then cook for another 15 minutes.
8. Serve with your favorite sides.

Salmon Pasta with Rosemary Tomato Sauce

Servings: 4
Cooking Time: 20 minutes
Calories: 440 kcal

Ingredients

    7 oz salmon fillet
    14 oz jar tomato pasta sauce
    3.5 oz parmesan cheese, grated
    3 garlic cloves, peeled and sliced
    1 large onion, peeled and chopped
    2 tomatoes, sliced
    2 slices of lemon
    2 fresh rosemary sprigs
    11 oz uncooked spaghetti
    6 cups water
    olive oil

salt and pepper, to taste

Instructions
1. Remove and chop the rosemary leaves. Cut two slices of lemon.
2. Put the salmon on a plate. Rub the fish with about 2 teaspoons pepper and the chopped rosemary. Put two slices of lemon on top.
3. Cover the fish and place in the fridge to marinade for at least 2 hours.
4. Preheat the air fryer to 320°F.
5. Add a splash of olive oil into the air fryer pan and cook the garlic for 3 minutes until golden brown.
6. Add onions, tomatoes and pasta sauce to the pan. Add some water and cook for 5 minutes.
7. Meanwhile boil water in a medium saucepan, add 1-2 teaspoons salt. Add pasta and cook for 7 minutes.
8. Remove the sauce from the air fryer and set aside.
9. Take the salmon out of the fridge and put into the air fryer. Cook for 10 minutes.
10. Using a fork break the cooked salmon into bite size pieces. Mix the cooked pasta and sauce together in a large bowl.
11. Split the pasta and sauce into 4 portions. Add a quarter of the cooked salmon to each portion, add grated parmesan.

12. Increase the temperature of the air fryer to 390°F. Put a pasta portion (one at a time) into the air fryer and cook for 2 minutes until the cheese has melted.
13. Bring the temperature down to 350°F. Cook for another 2 minutes.
14. Decrease the temperature to 320°F and cook for 4 minutes.

Shrimp Green Curry Noodles

Servings: 6
Cooking Time: 25 minutes
Calories: 271 per portion

Ingredients

    2 lb shirataki noodles
    12 big, cooked shrimp
    12 oz napa cabbage, base removed, leaves shredded
    12 oz extra firm tofu
    5 oz snow peas
    4 oz mushrooms, thinly sliced
    2 oz water chestnuts, peeled and sliced
    4 spring onions stalks, chopped
    2 carrots, peeled

1 red pepper, stems and seeds removed, thin-sliced

1 green pepper, stems and seeds removed, thin-sliced

6 tablespoons soy sauce

6 tablespoons thai green curry paste

4 tablespoons rice vinegar

3 tablespoons lime juice

1 ½ tablespoon fish sauce

2 teaspoons lemongrass paste

1 teaspoon sesame oil

1 teaspoon coriander paste

½ teaspoon garlic powder

Instructions

1. Preheat the air fryer to 350°F.
2. Rinse noodles with fresh water using a sieve. Put them into a big bowl and add 17 oz of boiling water. Add 1 tablespoon soy sauce and stir with a fork. Set aside.
3. Mix 3 tablespoons soy sauce with fish sauce, sesame oil and garlic powder in a medium bowl. Cut tofu into ½ inch size cubes and add into the sauce mix. Stir well to coat the tofu and set aside to marinade.
4. Grate carrots using the biggest grating surface. Separate vegetables and put cabbage, carrot and spring onions into one bowl, all other vegetables to another.

5. Take tofu out of its marinade with a slotted spoon. Make sure you keep the excess sauce. Spray/brush the cubes with a little oil and put them into the air fryer. Cook for 12-13 minutes until crispy.
6. Take tofu out of the air fryer and put on a plate. Cover to keep warm and set aside.
7. Spray/brush the shrimp with oil and put into the air fryer. Cook for 5 minutes.
8. Take the shrimp out and put on a plate, cover to keep warm.
9. Mix the leftover tofu marinade with 2 tablespoons rice vinegar and 2 tablespoons green curry paste in a small bowl. Pour the mixture into the air fryer along with all vegetables except cabbage, carrots and spring onions. Cook for 5 minutes.
10. Take another small bowl and make dressing by mixing coriander paste, lime juice and lemongrass paste with the remaining 4 tablespoons green curry paste and 2 tablespoons rice vinegar.
11. Drain the noodles and put them into one big bowl, then add dressing. Put tofu cubes on the top, cooked vegetables and the vegetable sauce.
12. Add fresh carrot, cabbage and spring onion mix, and then top with the shrimp to serve.

Salmon with Potatoes, Fennel and Dill

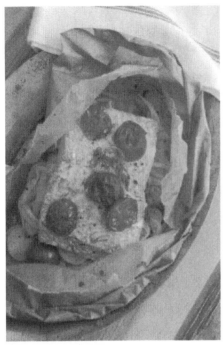

Servings: 2
Cooking Time: 20 minutes
Calories: 806 kcal

Ingredients

2 x 6 oz salmon fillets
8 cherry tomatoes
3 fingerling potatoes
½ fennel bulb
4 tablespoons butter

3 tablespoons dry vermouth (substitute with white wine or fish stock)
1 bunch fresh dill, leaves removed and chopped
3 cups water

Instructions

1. Preheat the air fryer to 400°F.
2. Wash and cut potatoes into ¼ inch thick slices. Cut the fennel bulb into ¼ inch thick slices. Halve cherry tomatoes.
3. Boil water in a medium saucepan, add 1-2 teaspoons salt. Put potato slices into the pan and cook for 2 minutes until they begin to soften. Drain and dry with a kitchen towel.
4. Cut two rectangles of parchment paper, roughly 13 x 15 inches. Melt butter in the microwave for about 15-20 seconds.
5. Put potatoes and fennel into a bowl and add half of melted butter. Add salt and black pepper and mix to combine.
6. Divide vegetables between two pieces of parchment and put them in the bottom. Add a pinch of dill onto each pile.
7. Put a fillet of salmon onto each pile of vegetables and season well with salt and pepper. Add cherry tomatoes to each portion on top of the salmon. Drizzle each portion with half of vermouth.

8. Fold the parchment paper so that the edges are all sealed.
9. Put two portions into the air fryer and cook for 15 to 20 minutes until the paper is puffed up and slightly brown. Check if the fish is cooked by making sure it is firm.
10. Serve immediately in the paper bags, garnished with fresh dill.

Rosemary Garlic Prawns

Servings: 2
Cooking Time: 7 minutes
Calories: 249 kcal

Ingredients

8 medium size prawns
4 garlic cloves, peeled and chopped
1 green or red pepper, stems and seeds removed, chopped
1 fresh rosemary sprig, leaves removed and chopped
½ tbsp butter
salt and pepper, to taste

79

Instructions

1. Melt butter in the microwave for about 15-20 seconds. Add garlic, rosemary, salt and pepper to butter. Stir well.
2. Put the prawns into a big bowl and pour the butter mixture over them. Stir well, cover and refrigerate for at least an hour to marinade.
3. Preheat the air fryer to 350°F.
4. Prepare 4 metal skewers. Thread the prawns and pepper chunks onto the skewers. Each skewer should have two prawns and at least two pieces of pepper.
5. Place the skewers into the air fryer. Cook for 6 minutes.
6. Turn the temperature up to 390°F. Cook for another 1 minute.
7. Serve with your favorite salads.

Black Cod

Servings: 2
Cooking Time: 15 minutes
Calories: 697 kcal

Ingredients

    2 fillets black cod

    7.2 oz kale, cut into strips

    3 oz grapes

    2.2 oz pecans

    1 small fennel bulb

    2 tablespoons extra virgin olive oil

    2 teaspoons white wine vinegar

    salt and pepper, to taste

1 tablespoon olive oil

Instructions
1. Preheat the air fryer to 400°F.
2. Rub the cod fillets with salt and pepper. Drizzle fish with a little olive oil.
3. Put the cod into the air fryer skin side down. Cook for 10 minutes.
4. Remove fish and set aside, cover it with tin foil.
5. Halve the grapes. Cut the fennel bulb into ¼ inch thick slices. Halve cherry tomatoes.
6. Put grapes, pecans and fennel into a bowl. Drizzle with a little olive oil and season well with salt and pepper. Put the mixture to the air fryer and cook for 5 minutes, stirring from time to time.
7. Put kale into a big bowl and add cooked grapes, pecans and fennel to it. Mix extra virgin olive oil and white wine vinegar in a smaller bowl. Pour the mixture over kale salad. Toss to coat.
8. Take the foil off the fish and serve with kale salad.

Cauliflower Burger

Servings: 8
Cooking Time: 20 minutes
Calories: 256 kcal

Ingredients

    2.2 lb cauliflower
    12 oz breadcrumbs
    1.6 oz oats
    1 small egg
    3 tablespoons plain flour
    3 teaspoons coconut oil
    3 teaspoons dried parsley
    2 teaspoons garlic paste
    2 teaspoons dried thyme

2 teaspoons dried chives
1 teaspoon mixed spice
1 teaspoon mustard powder
¼ teaspoon desiccated coconut
salt and pepper, to taste

Instructions

1. Take 8 oz of the breadcrumbs and put into a big bowl. Add 1 teaspoon dried parsley, 1 teaspoon salt and 1 teaspoon black pepper and mix well to combine. Cover and set aside for later.

2. Break the cauliflower into several florets. Boil ¼ inch of water in a big frying pan and add the cauliflower, add some salt. Cover and steam for 8 minutes.

3. Drain the cauliflower, and then use a sharp knife to dice it into very small pieces. Put it into blender, add mustard, 1 teaspoon garlic paste and a pinch of salt and pepper. Blend for a couple of minutes.

4. Drain the blended cauliflower and put it on a tea towel. Squeeze the towel to remove any excess liquid. Do this until the texture of cauliflower is like dough.

5. Put cauliflower into a big mixing bowl and add thyme, chives, mixed spice and coconut oil, along with the remaining 1 teaspoon garlic paste and 2 teaspoon parsley, salt and pepper. Mix well.

6. Add desiccated coconut, oats and all the remaining, plain breadcrumbs. Stir to combine.
7. Preheat the air fryer to 350°F.
8. Crack the egg into a medium bowl and whisk with a fork. Prepare the herbed breadcrumbs and spread some flour on a plate.
9. Dust your hands with flour so that the burger mixture doesn't stick to your skin. Form 8 burger patties out of cauliflower mixture.
10. Dip the patties in the flour and in the egg, coat them with herbed breadcrumbs.
11. Place the burgers into the air fryer and cook for 10 minutes. Flip and cook for another 10 minutes.
12. Serve with buns and salad.

Vegetable Pasta Salad

Servings: 8
Cooking Time: 1 hr 45 minutes
Calories: 121 kcal

Ingredients

 10 oz uncooked, mini farfalle pasta (or your choice)

 2 small eggplants

 2 small zucchini

 2 medium tomatoes

 1 bell pepper, seeds removed, chopped

 3.1 oz cherry tomatoes, cut in half

 2.5 oz parmesan, grated

 2 oz Italian salad dressing

 1 tablespoon olive oil

 2 teaspoons salt

 3 basil leaves

Instructions

1. Preheat the air fryer to 350°F.
2. Slice eggplants and zucchinis into ½ thick rounds. Spray/brush with a little oil.
3. Put the eggplant into the air fryer and cook for 15 minutes. Then, add zucchini and cook together for another 25 minutes until the vegetables are soft. Set aside.
4. Wash medium tomatoes and cut each tomato into 8 pieces. Spray/brush with oil and put into the air fryer. Cook for 30 minutes until reduced in size and a bit browned. Remove and set aside.
5. Boil a pan of salted water and cook pasta for 7 minutes. Drain pasta using a colander and then run under cold water. Drain again and set aside to cool.
6. Put a bell pepper and cherry tomatoes into a bowl.
7. Add cooked vegetables, pasta, 2 teaspoons salt, parmesan and dressing to the bowl. Toss with your hands to mix together.
8. Cover and put pasta salad into the fridge to chill before serving.

Buffalo Cauliflower

Servings: 4
Cooking Time: 15 minutes
Calories: 201 kcal

Ingredients

15 oz cauliflower (roughly one head)
4 oz panko breadcrumbs
2 oz butter
2 oz buffalo sauce
1 teaspoon sea salt

Instructions

1. Remove and discard cauliflower leaves. Cut the head into small pieces about 6 inches long.
2. Spread panko breadcrumbs on a plate and add some salt. Mix to combine, and then set aside.

3. Put butter into a mug and melt it in the microwave for 15-20 seconds. Add buffalo sauce.
4. Dip cauliflower heads into buffalo sauce mix, then into panko breadcrumbs until they are all well coated. Put them into the air fryer stacking vegetables if needed.
5. Do not preheat the air fryer. Once all the heads are in turn it on at 350°F. Cook for 14-17 minutes shaking from time to time. Keep an eye on the cauliflower to make sure it doesn't brown too much; they are done once they start browning and crisping up a little.
6. Serve with blue cheese dip.

Baked Sweet Potato

Servings: 3
Cooking Time: 40 minutes
Calories: 153 kcal

Ingredients

    3 sweet potatoes
    1 tablespoon olive oil
    2 teaspoons sea salt
    2 teaspoons black pepper
    1 ½ tablespoon butter

Instructions

1. Preheat the air fryer to 392°F.
2. Wash sweet potatoes. Use a fork to pierce the skin several times.
3. Drizzle potatoes with olive oil and add salt and pepper. Rub the seasoning and oil into potatoes ensuring they are evenly covered.
4. Put the potatoes into the air fryer basket and cook for 35-40 minutes until soften.
5. Cut and open the potatoes and top each with ½ tablespoon butter. Serve with your favorite toppings.

Pita Bread Pizza

Servings: 1
Cooking Time: 6 minutes
Calories: 347 kcal

Ingredients

 1 big, circular pita bread
 1 tablespoon pizza sauce
 2 oz mozzarella, grated
 ½ garlic clove, peeled and sliced
 ¼ onion, peeled and sliced
 1 tablespoon extra virgin olive oil
 2 basil leaves

Instructions

1. Preheat the air fryer to 350°F.
2. Spread the pizza sauce onto your pita bread using a spoon.
3. Add onion, garlic and cheese. If you want to add any other toppings add them before cheese. Drizzle with a little extra virgin olive oil.
4. Put the pita pizza into the air fryer and place a trivet over it. Cook for 6 minutes, until the cheese has melted and browned. Remove from the air fryer.
5. Put basil leaves on top.

Macaroni and Cheese

Servings: 2
Cooking Time: 35 minutes
Calories: 782 kcal

Ingredients

12 oz cheddar cheese, grated
8 oz milk
7 oz uncooked macaroni
2.5 oz broccoli
2 tablespoons parmesan cheese, grated
salt and pepper, to taste

Instructions

1. Preheat the air fryer to 390°F.
2. Cut the broccoli florets from the stalks. Cut them into small, equal size pieces.

3. Boil a medium size pan of salted water. Add macaroni and broccoli and reduce the heat to medium. Cook for 7-10 minute until both pasta and broccoli are cooked but not too soft. Drain and return to the pan.
4. Add milk, cheddar cheese, salt and pepper to macaroni. Stir well to combine.
5. Sprinkle parmesan over the top and put macaroni into the air fryer. Cook for 15 minutes until boiling.
6. Turn off the heat and leave pasta to sit in the air fryer for 5-10 minutes before serving.

Cabbage and Ginger Stir Fry

Servings: 4
Cooking Time: 25 minutes
Calories: 180 kcal

Ingredients

    14 oz cabbage, shredded
    5 oz frozen peas
    4 oz sweet onion, peeled and chopped
    1 red bell pepper, stems and seeds removed, chopped
    3 inch piece fresh ginger, peeled and chopped
    1 tablespoon olive oil
    1 teaspoon salt
    ½ teaspoon ground turmeric
    ½ teaspoon garam masala
    ½ teaspoon cayenne pepper
    4 oz water

Instructions

1. Preheat the air fryer to 350°F.
2. Mix salt, turmeric, garam masala and cayenne pepper in a small bowl. Set aside.
3. Put onion and ginger into the air fryer. Sprinkle with oil and cook for 5 minutes.
4. Add cabbage and peas to the air fryer along with the spice mix and water. Cook for 17 minutes.
5. Add the bell pepper and cook for another 3 minutes.
6. Serve with rice or noodles.

Quinoa Pilaf

Servings: 4
Cooking Time: 20 minutes
Calories: 333 kcal

Ingredients

    1 leek stalks, round sliced
    2 lemons
    2 garlic cloves, peeled and chopped
    1 block extra firm tofu
    6.2 oz frozen peas
    6 oz quinoa
    10 oz vegetable stock
    1 tablespoon olive oil

salt and pepper

Instructions
1. Heat oil in a big pan. Add leeks and cook for 5 minutes stirring frequently until soften.
2. Add quinoa and stir for another minute. Add vegetable stock. Bring to boil, then cover the pan and reduce the heat. Cook for 10 minutes.
3. Add peas to quinoa and cover the pan. Cook for 5 more minutes until quinoa is soft. Cover and set aside.
4. Meanwhile cut the tofu into ½ inch pieces. Grate the lemons rind and juice lemons into a small bowl.
5. Add lemon zest, garlic and a pinch of salt and pepper to lemon juice. Whisk to combine.
6. Put the tofu into a shallow dish and pour lemon sauce on it. Make sure the tofu is well coated, then set aside to marinade for 15 minutes.
7. Heat the air fryer to 370°F.
8. Put the tofu pieces into the air fryer basket using a slotted spoon, preserve the leftover marinade. Cook for 15 minutes shaking the basket every 8 minutes.
9. Take tofu out of the air fryer and serve with quinoa, drizzled with the leftover marinade.

Soy Vegetable Stir Fry

Servings: 4
Cooking Time: 25 minutes
Calories: 167 kcal

Ingredients

    5.3 oz green beans, both ends removed
    11.5 oz cauliflower
    4 mushrooms, halved
    3 sticks celery
    1 small onion, peeled and chopped
    1 medium carrot, peeled, thin-sliced
    1 bell pepper, stems and seeds removed, chopped
    3 tablespoons garlic soy sauce
    1 tablespoon olive oil
    salt and pepper, to taste

Instructions

1. Preheat the air fryer to 350°F.
2. Cut each bean into 3 pieces; remove and discard the cauliflower leaves and break the head into small florets. Remove and discard both ends of the celery, roughly chop the stalk.
3. Put carrots and onions into the air fryer and drizzle with oil. Season with salt and pepper, cook for 5 minutes.
4. Add green beans, cauliflower, celery and mushrooms. Cook for another 15 minutes.
5. Add bell pepper. Drizzle with the soy sauce and stir. Cook for 5 minutes.
6. Serve with rice or noodles.

Cauliflower Rice

Servings: 3
Cooking Time: 20 minutes
Calories: 153 kcal

Ingredients

11 oz riced cauliflower (you can buy pre-made
and skip the second step of the recipe)
½ block extra firm tofu
3.1 oz broccoli
2.6 oz frozen peas
2 carrots, peeled and chopped
2 garlic cloves, peeled and chopped
2 inch piece ginger, peeled and chopped

½ medium onion, peeled and chopped

1 teaspoon turmeric

4 tablespoons reduced sodium soy sauce

1 tablespoons rice vinegar

1 ½ teaspoon sesame oil

Instructions

1. Preheat the air fryer to 370°F.
2. Remove and discard the cauliflower leaves. If you have a blender, break the cauliflower head into florets and put into the blender. Pulse until thoroughly minced into pieces smaller than a pea. If you don't have a blender, you can use the biggest grating surface of your grater to make the cauliflower rice. Put aside.
3. Crumble the tofu into pieces in a separate bowl. Ideally it should resemble scrambled egg. Set aside.
4. Add carrots, onion, turmeric and 2 tablespoons soy sauce to the tofu. Mix and put into the air fryer. Cook for 10 minutes shaking once halfway through and remove from the air fryer once done.
5. Meanwhile remove the broccoli stem and chop the head into small pieces.
6. Put cauliflower rice into the bowl you used to mix the tofu. Add ginger, garlic, broccoli, peas, sesame oil, rice vinegar and the remaining 2 tablespoons soy sauce. Mix well.

7. Put the cauliflower mix into the air fryer (once the tofu has been removed). Cook for 10 minutes, shaking halfway through. The rice should be colored but not too brown.
8. Remove the cauliflower rice and toss together with the tofu mixture to serve.

Cinnamon doughnuts

Servings: 4
Cooking Time: 6 minutes
Calories: 345 kcal

Ingredients

    1 can premade, flaky biscuit dough

    3.5 oz granulated sugar

    1 tablespoon butter

    ½ tablespoon coconut oil

    1.5 teaspoon ground cinnamon

Instructions

1. Preheat the air fryer to 350°F.
2. Remove biscuits from the packet and put on a flat surface. Cut away the center of the biscuits to make doughnuts using a cookie cutter that is

1 inch in diameter. Reserve the dough from the middle.
3. Mix cinnamon and sugar in a medium bowl. You can add a pinch of black pepper for a stronger flavor.
4. Slightly grease the air fryer basket with coconut oil and place the doughnuts into the basket. Cook for 5-6 minutes until golden brown. You may also cook the dough from the middle for 3-4 minutes.
5. Meanwhile melt butter in the microwave for 15-20 seconds.
6. Brush the cooked doughnuts with melted butter and dip into the cinnamon mix to coat.

Carrot Cake

Servings: 8+
Cooking Time: 40 minutes
Calories: 252 kcal

Ingredients

> 5.3 oz self raising flour
>
> 4.2 oz carrots, peeled
>
> 4.1 oz light brown sugar
>
> 1.4 oz dried, mixed fruit
>
> 2 large eggs
>
> 6 tablespoons canola or vegetable oil
>
> 1 ½ tablespoon milk
>
> 1 teaspoon ground cinnamon
>
> 1 pinch salt

Instructions

1. Grate the carrot using the biggest grating surface of your grater. Set aside.

2. Mix flour and cinnamon in a big bowl. Set aside.
3. In a separate bowl crack the eggs and beat slightly using a fork. Add sugar and beat (either using an electric mixer or a hand whisk) until combined.
4. Add milk, oil and a pinch of salt to the egg mixture. Stir gently.
5. Pour the egg mixture into the flour bowl. Using a spatula or a wooden spoon stir gently until combined.
6. Add carrots and mixed fruits, continue to stir. Add the next portion only when the previous one has been well combined.
7. Preheat the air fryer to 356°F.
8. Pour the cake mixture into the baking pan and cover with tin foil. Make small holes in the foil to allow the air in.
9. Put the pan into the air fryer and reduce the temperature to 320°F. Cook for 35 minutes.
10. Remove the foil and continue to cook for another 3-5 minutes until the surface of the cake is firm and golden brown and a skewer inserted into the cake comes out clean.
11. Allow to cool before serving.

Cinnamon Rolls

Servings: 10
Cook Time: 25 minutes
Calories: 492 kcal

Ingredients

 1.5 lb plain flour
 8.4 oz milk
 3.9 oz butter
 1.9 oz sugar, plus 1 tbsp extra
 2 ¼ teaspoons rapid rise yeast
 1 ½ teaspoon ground cinnamon
 ¼ teaspoon salt
 canola oil

For the glaze:
>   4 oz cream cheese
>   4.4 oz powdered sugar
>   ½ stick unsalted butter
>   ½ teaspoon vanilla extract

Instructions

1. Heat milk and 3 tablespoons of butter on a medium heat in a big saucepan. Do not let the mixture boil; it just needs to be warm enough for butter to melt.
2. Remove the pan from the heat and allow it to cool to 104°F (you can measure using a kitchen thermometer). It needs to be warm but not too hot as the excessive heat can kill the yeast.
3. Pour the cooled mixture into a big mixing bowl and add the yeast. Leave for 10 minutes and allow the yeast to activate.
4. Add 1 tablespoon sugar and ¼ teaspoon salt and stir.
5. Add the flour slowly, sieving in ⅙ at a time and stirring as you do. The dough will begin to get stickier as you add more flour. Eventually, it will become too thick to stir. Then sprinkle a little flour onto your worktop and put the dough on it.
6. Knead for a minute or so until the dough forms a smooth, loose ball. Rinse out the bowl you used to mix the dough, then dry and coat with

the oil. Place the dough ball back into the bowl and cover with plastic wrap. Put the bowl in a warm, dry place and leave the dough to rise for an hour.

7. Once the dough has risen take it out and put on a lightly floured surface. Use a rolling pin to roll the dough out into a thin rectangle.

8. Melt 3 tablespoons butter in the microwave for 15-20 seconds. Brush the butter onto the flattened dough, and then sprinkle with 1.9 oz sugar and up to 1 tablespoon ground cinnamon (depending on how strong you would like the flavor to be).

9. Starting at the shortest edge, tightly roll up the dough and seal edges. Once rolled, put it on your work surface seam side down.

10. Using a sharp knife or string floss cut the dough into 2 inch sections. Butter a round pan and place the rolls into the pan, cinnamon swirl side up. You should be able to make around 10 rolls.

11. Melt the remaining 2 tablespoons butter in the microwave for 15-20 seconds, and brush it over the rolls. Cover the rolls with plastic wrap.

12. Preheat the air fryer to 356°F. Take the cream cheese and butter for the glaze out of the refrigerator.

13. Remove the plastic wrap and place the roll pan into the air fryer. Cook for 25-30 minutes until

golden brown. Remove from the air fryer and allow cooling for a few minutes.

14.Meanwhile put the cream cheese, powdered sugar, butter and vanilla extract into a bowl. Beat until smooth using an electric mixer.

15.Spread the glaze onto the slightly cooled cinnamon rolls and enjoy immediately.

Chocolate Muffins

Servings: 12
Cooking Time: 15 minutes
Calories: 338 kcal

Ingredients

12.3 oz self raising flour

8.8 oz milk

6.3 oz chocolate chips

5.3 oz brown sugar

4.4 oz unsalted butter

1.8 oz unsweetened cocoa powder

2 medium eggs

Instructions

1. Preheat the air fryer to 320°F.
2. Sieve the flour and cocoa powder into a big mixing bowl. Add brown sugar and chocolate chips and stir well to combine.

3. Melt the butter in the microwave for 15-20 seconds, and then allow cooling for a couple of minutes. Crack the eggs into a medium bowl, add milk and melted butter. Whisk until well combined.
4. Pour the egg mixture into the flour mixture. Stir with a spatula or a wooden spoon until combined. Make sure you don't over mix.
5. Arrange 12 muffin cases in a muffin pan that will fit in the air fryer. Put the mixture into the cases until they are ¾ full.
6. Place the muffins into the air fryer and cook for 13-15 minutes until firm and a skewer inserted into the center comes out clean.
7. Cook for a couple of minutes more, transfer to wire rack to cool.

Banana Fritters

Servings: 8
Cooking Time: 10 minutes
Calories: 204 kcal

Ingredients

8 Pisang raja bananas, or other small bananas

1 egg white

3 oz breadcrumbs

3 tablespoons corn flour

3 tablespoons vegetable oil

Instructions

1. Heat vegetable oil in a pan or skillet. Add breadcrumbs and fry for a few minutes until golden. Put on a plate and set aside.
2. Preheat the air fryer to 356°F.

3. Peel the bananas, remove and discard the bottom. Put the corn flour on a plate.
4. Dip the peeled bananas into corn flour then in the egg white and roll in the breadcrumbs until well covered.
5. Put the bananas into the air fryer basket. DO NOT STACK. Cook for 8 minutes until the outside of the bananas is golden and crispy.
6. Remove from the air fryer and drain on a kitchen towel. Serve warm.